THE MEN
WITH
BARE
FEET

THE MEN WITH BARE FEET

Discovering Intimacy
With God Through
Moses, Joshua,
and Jesus

JORDAN LOFTIS

THRONE
PUBLISHING GROUP

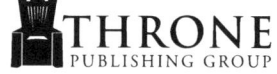

Jordan unpacks some of the familiar stories about Moses, Joshua and Jesus in a way that is not only fresh but applicable. Whether you are new to faith or you have been following Christ for years, you will greatly enjoy reading (and understanding) how our intimacy with God makes all the difference in the world.

Tom Henderson, Author of *Heart Not Hype*
and Founder/Speaker of Restoration Generation

The Men With Bare Feet will compel you to draw close to the God who burns and battles for his people, yet also washes their feet. Through the lives of Moses, Joshua, and Jesus, Jordan helps us see God in both his glory and nearness. I highly recommend you read this book and follow its author, as this is the first of many excellent teachings from this mighty man of faith.

Jeremy D. Brown, Author of
Warrior: How God Makes Mighty Men
and Founder of Warrior Leadership

I've known Jordan for over ten years, and have been privileged to see him grow into the man of God he is today. He walks what he talks. So, if you've ever struggled with feeling close to God through His word or prayer, read this book.

Ryan Bell,
Creator of shortdailydevotions.com

Copyright © 2017 by Jordan Loftis

ISBN: 978-1-945255-37-3

All rights reserved. No part of this book may be reproduced or transmitted in any form or by any means, electronic or mechanical, including photocopying, recording or by any information storage and retrieval system, without permission in writing from the copyright owner. For information on distribution rights, royalties, derivative works or licensing opportunities on behalf of this content or work, please contact the publisher at the address below.

Printed in the United States of America.

Although the author and publisher have made every effort to ensure that the information and advice in this book was correct and accurate at press time, the author and publisher do not assume and hereby disclaim any liability to any party for any loss, damage, or disruption caused from acting upon the information in this book or by errors or omissions, whether such errors or omissions result from negligence, accident, or any other cause.

Scripture quotations are from the ESV® Bible (The Holy Bible, English Standard Version®), copyright © 2001 by Crossway, a publishing ministry of Good News Publishers.
Used by permission. All rights reserved.

Cover and book design by Tim Murray | paperbackdesign.com
Text is set in 11/15 Mrs. Eaves / Mr. Eaves, by Zuzana Licko—1996

Throne Publishing Group
2329 N Career Ave #215
Sioux Falls, SD 57107
ThronePG.com

PREFACE
xi

PART ONE: MOSES

ONE: THE WOVEN ARK
1

TWO: REVELATION IN FLAME
9

THREE: THE BRIDEGROOM OF BLOOD
19

PART TWO: JOSHUA

FOUR: THE MOUNTAINSIDE APPRENTICE
35

FIVE: WORSHIP AS WARFARE
45

SIX: CLINGING TO GOD
53

PART THREE: JESUS

SEVEN: THE SERVANT'S BASIN
65

EIGHT: LIVING WITH BARE FEET
71

ABOUT THE AUTHOR
79

NOTES
81

To Fallon,
for rekindling Daddy's wonder beneath
a sea of stars.

PREFACE

On a recent wintry night, my daughter and I had just returned home. She's about two years old and is just getting the hang of words, so each new phrase she learns still sends shockwaves of delight through my body.

I wrangled her out of the car seat, and as I closed the car door, she pointed upward, gasping, "Stars, stars!" I followed her little finger, and there was Orion, blazing in the sky. She couldn't get over all of them and cried to stay outside in the cold to look at them.

We stayed and looked.

I'll never forget her absolute awe at God's brilliant creation—it's infectious. At that moment, I wished she was old enough to look through a telescope. There's nothing like seeing clutches of star dust sprinkled across the nighttime sky. Galaxies upon galaxies hanging motionless, telling the story of ages gone by. Jupiter and Venus reflecting the sun's light back to earth, bright as any star.

In a way, I hope this book is a telescope for you. Telescopes make massive, glorious, far-away things seem close up. And I hope the incredible stories we're about to explore from the lives of Moses, Joshua, and Jesus are brought close. They hold so much value for us because they are both true and part of our heritage. We must never forget who we are.

LEARNING WHO WE ARE

Have you ever met someone with Alzheimer's disease or dementia? It's heartbreaking to watch, especially if you knew them before their decline. For me, it seems like they're slowly being erased from the world, like an old sketch on a chalkboard. One swipe after the next makes them disturbingly vanish, leaving behind smudges of who they once were.

You see, our identity is rooted in our memory, and if you can't remember, you can't know who you are. What's unnerving about these awful diseases is that people seem to die before they're ever really gone. They look you in the eyes but without any light of recognition or shared love.

Today, we often suffer from a kind of spiritual amnesia when God's Word fades like a flag left too long in the sun. When we forget the Biblical exploits, narratives, and revelations, we don't simply lose an opportunity to know God's heart, we become disconnected from our identities.

Just like being divorced from our personal memories if we were sick, we forget who we really are. I'm not just

PREFACE

a twenty-something guy named Jordan—I'm an adopted son of the Father of Lights. That reality poorly resonates if I lack a deep sense of what it means.

The Apostle Paul writes: "So faith comes from hearing, and hearing through the word of Christ" (Romans 10:17). This book is an invitation for us to "hear" God's Word together so that our faith is increased and our identities are strengthened. It's an exploration of more than neat history, it's a piece of our origin story as disciples of Jesus.

To know who we are means to look at who our God is. Instead of revealing Himself primarily through monotonous rules and laws, He shows us His character by how He interacts with His people. We see God's nature and personality and meet Him just as His people did. Remember, our God hasn't changed. So when we discover who He was, He reveals who He is. My hope is that you meet God with me in this book and discover the power of knowing Him.

If you only remember one thing, make it this: Eternal life is not a far away place called heaven, but a relationship with its King. So join me in peering through the telescope to see God with a fresh perspective. Our lens will be the stories of Moses, Joshua, and Jesus—the men with bare feet.

PART ONE

MOSES

ONE

THE WOVEN ARK

Water lapped against the brave little river boat. It was handwoven from Egyptian bulrushes for a special mission and sealed against the waves. Its cargo was just big enough to fill the tiny hull as it bobbed up and down, hidden among the reeds. These were dangerous waters, though.

Crocodiles lurked and poisonous snakes slithered like ribbons through the current. This was not a safe place. Yet it was the only refuge for a baby boy named Moses. His basket boat was made of papyrus reeds, what the ancient Egyptians used to make their paper. Here, in the morning sun, he became the opening lines in one of God's most incredible stories.

In the beginning of Exodus, we read about Israel's slavery. Egypt had a new king, and he decided that the Israelites were becoming too many to control. So, he leveled

THE MEN WITH BARE FEET

two evil orders against them. First, he made them slaves and put ruthless taskmasters in charge. Men with whips, clubs, and power loomed over them, berating, beating, and driving them to the brink of exhaustion. A funny thing happened, though. No matter how hard the taskmasters pressed the people, they grew stronger and had more children. Even though the slave drivers made their lives bitter—*their hands torn apart by bricks, their backs broken in desert heat*—these were miraculously tough people, with bodies made of stone harder than the bricks they were forced to make.

The king, also called a Pharoah, laid out a second order that was more horrifying than the first. It decreed that their midwives were to murder every infant son straight from the womb (Ex. 2:16). This massacre took place on the banks of the mighty Nile River. Teeming with danger, it devoured Israel's sons whole. They were drowned, their innocent cries muffled by the rapids.

DRAWN OUT

From the second she saw him, Moses's mother knew he was something special (Ex. 2:2). So she hid him for three months. Can you imagine hiding a baby who cried and needed constant care? Moses was born to brave parents who weren't going to give in to the wicked king. But the Egyptians closed in. Each day, they were nearer to finding him (Ex. 2:3). She realized it was now or never if Moses had any chance to live.

Steeling her nerves, she wound through the streets with her daughter, Moses's older sister, Miriam, with his makeshift basket tucked beneath her arm. She prayed and clenched her teeth, counting the steps to the banks of the river. Miriam played lookout while their mother set him adrift. Her tears dappled the water as she gently pushed him from shore, leaving behind a shallow wake. Her stomach was in knots, but he was in God's hands now. While Moses's tiny countrymen met a grim fate, he floated atop the tomb in secret. This young boy would change the world forever, and the ruthless Pharaoh's daughter would help him do it (Ex. 2:10).

That morning, the princess went to the river and heard him crying. She knew he was an Israelite boy and condemned to die, but she pitied him and turned to Miriam who still stood by. The princess said to her, "Take this child away and nurse him for me, and I will give you your wages" (Ex. 2:9). Ironically, the princess gave him an Egyptian name that sounds like the Hebrew word for "draw out." So that's exactly what she did. Miriam's heart must've leapt for joy! The plan worked. Her little brother would be safe and nursed by their own mother. Not only safe, but he would grow up a prince as part of the royal family.

You just can't beat this turn of events.

FLIGHT TO MIDIAN

The book of Exodus doesn't give us much about Moses's growing up years. All we know is that four decades slip by. And when we find him next, our basket-born baby is a grown man beginning to feel the pull of his Hebrew roots. Right after the princess names him, we read, "One day, when Moses had grown up, he went out to his people and looked on their burdens, and he saw an Egyptian beating a Hebrew, one of his people" (Ex. 2:11) This verse tells us *twice* that Moses saw the plight of "his people." Though he was an Egyptian prince, his heart ached for them.

He'd certainly noticed their pain and suffering before, but something about this time was different. He *went out* to survey how difficult the Hebrew people's lives were. One event stood apart from the rest and became the next big turning point in his life. An Egyptian was beating an Israelite, which evoked a new level of rage inside of him. He saw the cruelty and couldn't pass by. So, he glanced to see if anyone else was around. The streets around him were empty, so he charged the oppressor and beat him to death. He made a decision in blood to side with his people over the ones who'd raised him. And he then buried the dead Egyptian's body in the sand, covering his crime (Ex. 2:12).

Moses became an avenger for his people, but something unexpected happened. The next day, he went back on patrol. Instead of seeing an Egyptian and an Israelite in a scuffle, he saw two Israelites in a fist fight. He intervened here, too, asking the man who started it, "Why do you strike your companion?" (Ex. 2:13). The man immediately quipped, "Who made you a prince and a judge over us? Do you mean to kill me as you killed the Egyptian?" (Ex. 2:14). Moses's stomach flopped upside down. He thought there were no witnesses, but this man threw the killing right back in his face. This did two things in Moses.

First, it was a rejection of his intervention. I can hear the sarcasm in the man's use of his royal Egyptian title of "prince" and "judge." He spat more venom by insinuating Moses was going to kill him just like he did the Egyptian. To this man, it was as if Moses acted in senseless wrath, not as a protector and defender—not as *one of them*. Moses's first recorded action for the deliverance of his people is met with rejection and skepticism. This planted seeds that would germinate over forty years, as we'll observe in chapter three.

Second, it also turned his nerves to jelly. We get a view into his panicked thoughts, and he thinks, "Surely this thing is known" (Ex. 2:14). He was right. The Pharaoh caught wind of Moses's crime against Egypt and dispatched soldiers to kill him. He had to pay retribution and come down with an iron fist. Remember, Pharaoh was leery of the Hebrews. They prospered even under slavery. Moses needed to be made into an example. No exceptions, even for an adopted royal.

So, Moses does the logical thing: he runs! He flees to a region called Midian, which was located on the other side of the Red Sea from Egypt. If you imagine a map, Egypt is on the western shore of the sea, which is a long, narrow body of water running North to South. And Midian is on the eastern shore (in what is modern day Saudi Arabia).

Moses escapes the king's clutches, and danger seems to be far behind—until he arrives in Midian. Tired from running, and probably relieved, he sits by a well. Only his nature as a protector flares up again, and he jumps into the middle of another fray. He's sitting at the well, drinking some water amid the arid surroundings, when bandit-like shepherds burst into view. They're attacking

THE MEN WITH BARE FEET

seven sisters, chasing them and the flock they tended. We don't know how many shepherds there were, but evidently not enough to take on a battle-tested Moses. He swoops in, saves the sisters, and then waters their flock (Ex. 2:16-17).

A WIFE, A BABY, AND FORTY YEARS

Moses is a defender, savior, and fighter to his core. He's not afraid of a scrape, especially when the weak are overrun by the strong. He had a shepherd's temperament. So, that's what he did in Midian for the next forty years—but not before marrying one of the seven sisters he'd just rescued. Her name was Zipporah, and in just a few verses, they have a baby boy named Gershom, a name that sounds like the Hebrew word for "sojourner."

In the span of a few days, Moses went from royal fugitive to the shepherd of his new father-in-law's flock. He lived a quiet life for four decades there, until a meeting took place that doubled down on his roots as the guardian of Israel. While Moses lived the pastoral life, however, the people back in Egypt suffered more and more. But "God heard their groaning... and God remembered His covenant with Abraham... [and] saw the people of Israel—and God knew" (Ex. 2:25).

That final line sends shivers down my spine. *God knew.* He saw the Egyptian cruelty. He heard the people's screams. He saw the river of tears they shed. The first forty years of Moses's story is bookended by his people in despair. Their infant sons mercilessly murdered, and their oppression growing more insidious by the year. From the beginning, though, God is orchestrating something. He's not forgotten His centuries-old promise to the father of the Israelites, Abraham. In these first pages of Exodus, we see Moses's nature on display. But we also see God's.

God knew.

TWO

REVELATION IN FLAME

Few things are better than a campfire. The crackle and pop of logs. Licks of flame dancing with one another. The shifting strata of orange, yellow, and blue providing heat on chilly nights.

My favorite place for campfires is somewhere deep in the mountains or forest, where the tree trunks glow and the firelight fades into the dark wilds beyond our ring of light. Then, as midnight creeps closer, and we're ready to tuck ourselves into tents and sleeping bags, the conversation grows quiet.

We watch the fire burn down to coals in silence, reflecting on the day. Feeling our muscles ache from hiking, climbing, and catching trout. Remembering the sweeping meadows, steep canyons, and serene lakes.

If you've ever looked intently at the coals of a dying fire, you know how veins of heat progress across their surface. They look like molten lava, pulsing with light. Melodramatic as it is, I've always felt like I was staring into eternity watching the coals of a campfire grow dim. There's just something about a fire in the mountains that makes you ponder life's big questions and mysteries. There is one fire in the mountains, however, that stands apart from the rest in all the history of mankind.

A FRESH PERSPECTIVE

Christian or not, most Americans have heard the story of the burning bush. We read about it in Exodus 3 and 4. Like so many of the greatest Bible stories, though, it can become dim like a dying campfire. We lose its heat, power, and relevance when we've heard it so many times. As we look at it together in this chapter, do your best to put on fresh glasses.

Start by putting yourself in Moses's sandals. Picture walking in the desert mountains. Feel the intensity of the flames. Wonder at the miracle burning right in front of you. Marvel that somehow, some way, and for some reason, the God who simply spoke and made the universe has appeared on a remote mountainside. He's speaking to you, and you alone at this moment in space and time.

It can be challenging, but when you approach stories like this in the Bible, remember a few things. First and foremost: *this really happened*. This isn't a fairytale, fable, or fantasy to be shared around the campfire. It's not a myth, it's history. If you had been peeking over a ridge, watching Moses traipse among the foothills, you would have seen this incredible sight.

Second, this story is not just an incredible event unrelated to your life here and now. It's part of your heritage. Through Jesus, we're related to Moses as one of our fathers. He's our spiritual ancestor, a part of our lineage. When we read about his encounter with God, we're reading about *our* encounter with God in a sense. God didn't simply reveal Himself to Moses, he revealed Himself to all of us who would treasure this moment and soak it up.

Third, this is also a critical moment in the Bible itself. We only see a few events like this in the Old Testament, but in this book, we'll look at two others in parts two and three when we get to Joshua and Jesus. This story is something theologians call a *theophany*. Basically, it means that the invisible God is revealing Himself in a visible way. When this happens, it's like a sentence in all caps with a thousand exclamation points and one-thousand-point font. It's something so important that it can't be missed if we are to know who God is.

Now, let's approach the flames with Moses, and meet God anew.

THE TALKING FLAMES

We return to Moses's story in Exodus 3. At this point, he's living in the wilderness as a shepherd with his wife, two sons, and family. We learn later in the book of Exodus that Moses and Zipporah had a second son named Eliezer, whose name memorialized God saving him from Pharaoh [Ex. 18:4]. But today was just another average day in Moses's quiet life.

He "led his flock to the west side of the wilderness" (Ex. 3:1). As he walked along, however, something marvelous caught his eye. He saw a "bush that was burning, yet... not consumed" (Ex. 3:2). Moses immediately runs to "see this great sight" and investigate why the bush was on fire yet "not burned" (Ex. 3:3).

I've enjoyed hundreds of campfires, but have yet to see one like this. Here, Moses stumbles onto a thorny bramble bush, wreathed in flames, yet not the least bit singed. His flock continues to mill about as he steps away, probably scratching his head.

Then it happens. A voice thunders from the miraculous bush, "Moses, Moses!" Astounded, he replies, "Here I am." In effect, he's simply saying, "Yes, what would you like from me, mystery flaming bush?" But before the voice tells him what he wants, he sounds a warning: "Do not come near; take your sandals off your feet, for the place on which you are standing is holy ground" (Ex. 3:5).

You see, God's first order of business wasn't to get Moses's attention; it was to save him. Moses's curiosity was piqued and he quickly approached the burning bush. God had to stop him before he came any closer, however. Because if Moses came too near, he likely would have died.

This might be a bit confusing, but we learn a lot about God in His conversation with Moses. There are five main things I'll draw your attention to, the first being His holiness. God's very first words are a warning to Moses to keep his distance. Why? Because of his holiness.

GOD'S HOLINESS

Immediately after telling him to stay back, God tells him to go barefoot, because he stood on holy ground. We hear a lot about God's holiness. It's a familiar phrase in the Bible, in sermons, and even in our worship songs. Here, we learn that it's much more than a theological term. God's holiness isn't something for text books and Sunday school, it's *deathly serious*.

God's holiness is more than his moral righteousness and perfection, though they are a part of it. Instead, it's His "set apartness." God is something completely different in nature than we are. While we bear His image, we do not hold His qualities. His holiness is so potent and palpable that it can actually kill. Our bodies can't stand up under its weight. Its magnitude overwhelms us so much, that it puts us to death. Just like a raging inferno, if we encounter God's holiness without being utterly holy ourselves, we won't live to talk about the encounter.

Think about it like this. Fire consumes everything it touches except for other flames. When it's hot enough, it melts stone and evaporates water. When flame meets flame, however, they intertwine and become one. When like meets like, things are okay. When like meets different, though, the stronger dominates the weaker. This is how it works with God's holiness, and the flames represent this reality. So when God calls out, "Moses, Moses!" it isn't in simple greeting. It's an urgent warning to stay in the safety zone God had prepared.

Whenever we read about God's holiness, we should think about this scene. We should remember the flames, the warning, and the unapproachable light of God (1 Tim. 6:16). It means He is of a different quality and substance than us. Eternal. Perfect.

And overwhelmingly powerful on a massive scale.

THE MEN WITH BARE FEET

GOD'S CONSUMING PRESERVATION

However, there is a twin truth here. God's presence is preserving even as it's consuming. He has wreathed the bush in flames, yet it isn't burned to a crisp. In this moment, God is also signaling his willingness to draw near in His power for the sake of preservation.

It's a foreshadowing of how He will lead his people from bondage in Egypt. His holiness will descend and deliver them, yet protect their lives. And through Moses, he will also reveal the Law so that the people can be in right relationship with Himself. Moses's character as a guardian was obviously developed by God Himself.

GOD'S GLORY

This experience, wonderful as it was, was also terrifying for Moses. After God spoke to him, we read that Moses "hid his face, for he was afraid to look at God" (Ex. 3:6). When he realized who spoke to him and what was happening, he felt the weight of God's glory. For along with God's holiness, His unique glory was also represented by the flame. We see an image painted of God's glory that likens it to a one-of-a-kind inferno. It cannot be missed. It cannot be mistaken. Simply put, there is nothing like it.

In Exodus 33, when Moses is with God on the summit of this very mountain, he will again be speaking to the God who is a "consuming fire" (Deut. 4:24; Heb. 12:29). In that awe-inspiring scene, he asks God, "Please show me your glory" (Ex. 33:18). In response, God makes all of his goodness pass before Moses and proclaims again to him His name.

There's a marvelous nuance here that is the central vein of this book. Moses's intimate encounter with God at the burning bush would later transform his fear into longing. A desire to see God's glory once again manifested. To gaze at His beauty. To know Him more fully. He held the gaze and attention of the eternal I AM, and shares his deepest desire. Moses wanted to behold God in His glory.

When our eyes are enamored by God's face and our souls hungry for His presence, we find our greatest joy. It's the reason we were made. If you remember one thing from this book, make it this: Eternal life is not a place called heaven, it's a relationship with its King. As Jesus would echo more than 1,500 years later: "And this is eternal life, that they know you the only true God, and Jesus Christ whom you have sent. I glorified you on earth, having accomplished the work that you gave me to do. And now, Father, glorify me in your own presence with the glory that I had with you before the world existed" (Jn. 17:3-5).

GOD'S PROMISE

Even as Moses shields himself, though, God continues to speak. He says in Exodus 3:7-8: "I have surely seen the affliction of my people who are in Egypt and have heard their cry because of their taskmasters. I know their sufferings, and I have come down to deliver them out of the hand of the Egyptians and to bring them up out of that land to a good and broad land, a land flowing with milk and honey…"

First, we learn that when God's people suffer, he sees. Just like King David wrote of God's character in Psalm

34:15, "The eyes of the LORD are toward the righteous and his ears toward their cry." God came down to be with His people in a tangible way. He came to lead them from slavery and into His presence. He reveals the same nature Jesus would embody. He's the deliverer who draws near to His people.

Second, we find something else we often take for granted. God is also claiming them as his own people. They're not *some people*, they're *His people*. He's fulfilling His promise to Abraham in Genesis 12:1-3, that He would make him into a "great nation." This great nation was God's own possession. They were also going to inherit a good land, which we'll learn more about in chapter six.

GOD'S ESSENCE

Moses responds with concerns. First doubting his own credibility, and second, the very identity of the God presenting Himself. He knew of the God of Abraham, Isaac, and of Jacob. But He was *their* God. If they were His people, wasn't He also the people's God today? Moses wanted a name, just like the Egyptian gods had names. But instead of a mere name, he got an identity, a personality: *God Himself*.

In response to Moses's question, God utters words that shake the foundation of the world: "I AM WHO I AM" (Ex. 3:14). God reveals His essence to Moses, and rather than giving Himself a descriptor of mere words, he illustrates his nature. "I exist." This is the first time in all of Scripture that God reveals Himself so intimately and explicitly. God wasn't side-stepping the question of His name, He went deeper.

REVELATION IN FLAME

"I AM" is connected with the Hebrew verb *hayah*, which means "to be." He is the uncreated Creator. The God who exists eternally, without beginning or end. He is unbound by space and time, and yet, His nature is also *to be with His people*. He is the God too holy to approach on our terms, yet closes the gap and draws near.

The name I AM is Yahweh (YWHW in Hebrew). And every time you see the word "LORD" in all caps in the Bible, that signifies this special name revealed to Moses from the burning bush. This name that signifies God's eternal essence and tender heart to be with His people.

At this point, Moses's mind must be swimming. But, as we'll see, those seeds of doubt planted forty years earlier when he ran from Egypt have sprouted. Even though he's standing before an unprecedented miracle, his first instinct is to respond to God in a different sort of fear than he felt at God's presence. Rather than a holy awe and barefooted reverence, he's scared of what people will think.

Something that plagues us all.

THREE

THE BRIDEGROOM OF BLOOD

Exodus 4 is wild on a few levels. Moses is still bowed low before a bush consumed by flames yet hasn't burned. He not only met the God of the Universe, he spoke with Him. In this chapter, we see God proving that Moses wouldn't be going it alone. He'd be stamped with the authority of the Creator. It wasn't Moses's cunning power or eloquence that would win the day. It would be God's. However, this isn't how Moses saw it.

He was afraid.

God promised to strike Egypt with wonders and even cause them to hand over their jewels, gold, and silver willingly to the slaves as they made their getaway. He also promised Moses something stunning, that the elders of Israel would listen to his voice (Ex. 3:18). This theme will repeat itself. Godly leaders are made by God Himself. He sets them up, grants them authority, and shows them what to do. All they need to do is obey. Total obedience was the character of leadership God was about to work into Moses.

As we'll see, though, Moses saw God's charge in a dimmer light. His attitude wasn't first one of faith but of reluctance. God gave him the keychain to unlock the shackles that hung around his people's neck. But Moses's response was, "What good is a key if you can't find the lock?"

In this chapter, we'll look at three reluctances Moses had to God's commands. The first was that he thought the people would think he's a fraud; people don't follow those they don't trust. The second was that he wasn't an inspiring communicator—a pretty important trait for a leader. And the third was an old act of disobedience that needed taken care of. To start, let's listen in as Moses explains to God why he's simply not the right man for the job.

FIRST RELUCTANCE: CREDIBILITY

At this point in his life, Moses's greatest fear is what people think of him. This seems laughable, doesn't it? Could you imagine standing in front of a bush, totally ablaze, yet not in the least bit singed? And then, even more incredibly, it starts talking to you! No matter where you're from, stuff like this just doesn't happen. With eyes aglow before this burning miracle, he says: "The people are never going to believe me."

This is a classic Debbie-downer moment. He doesn't ask God if the people doubt his credibility. This sentence doesn't end with a question mark. It ends with a period. It's a flat statement: "God, people are never going to believe me." He's ready to throw in the shepherd's cloak before he even begins. However, God was patient with him and answered his fears.

"What's in your hand?" God asked.

"My staff," Moses replied.

"Throw it on the ground," God commanded.

We then read, "So he threw it on the ground, and it became a serpent, and Moses ran from it" (Ex. 4:3). The instant his staff hit the dust, it writhed to life and headed straight for him. He ran for it, but God said, " 'Put out your hand and catch it by the tail'—so he put out his hand and caught it, and it became a staff in his hand..." (Ex. 4:4).

This is an interesting turn. Moses was understandably scared and ran from the mystical—*yet very real*—snake. However, the moment God commanded him to grab the object of his fear, he obeyed. His reluctance to trust in God didn't come from fear of danger. After all, he'd fought and killed the Egyptian beating his countryman (Ex. 2:12) and even defended Zipporah and her sisters from violent shepherds (Ex. 2:17). He wasn't a coward when it came to action. What scared Moses most is *what people thought of him*.

WHAT I FEAR MOST

Now, there aren't many places in life I'd compare myself to Moses, but this is one of them. I've always liked doing intense, and moderately dangerous, things. I've free climbed buildings that are stories high (don't you dare do this), and actually broke my back jumping off one of them. I've rappelled ranger-style down cliff faces (probably don't do this, either), which means that instead of gliding down backward, you run down the cliff face first. It's intense; especially the time when my harness broke.

Growing up, if my friends and I were going to do something dangerous, I always went first. Obviously someone at the factory forgot to tighten all the screws in my brain before they let me leave. But as a man, there's still something in me that craves danger. Scaling buildings, climbing cliffs, bombing trails mountain biking... and the list goes on. My no-guts-no-glory attitude in these areas, though, don't translate into where I'm most afraid.

I've been preaching and teaching the Bible since I was about twelve years old. And despite the wild, adrenaline-addicted streak in me, I've always been scared most of what people think of me. Isn't that silly? I've taken tons of needless, stupid risks that put my life in real danger. Yet people's opinion of me is what keeps me up at night. A desire to be liked and praised has dominated lots of my life. Succumbing to the fear of embarrassment has left me with some deep regrets. From opportunities to share the Gospel that I let pass by to giving into peer pressure and doing pretty rank things.

Through this, I've learned that the degree to which you let people's opinions influence you is the ceiling on your potential as a leader. If you're controlled by fear, you won't be brave. Notice I didn't say, "If you fear..." I said, "If you're controlled" by it. This kind of living is toxic because it keeps you from becoming who you truly are in Christ. Just like Moses was doing, you look to people's approval rather than God's. However, God does something spectacular with our fear when we listen to Him.

His response to it is astounding, comforting, challenging, and assuring all at once. He tells you to throw down your strength, and He turns it into something dangerous. He shows that while you see a simple wooden stick, he sees a coiled viper ready to strike. It's not about what you are. It's about who He is.

This is a promise we read throughout the Bible, and one we find in this scene on the mountain. God tells Moses that He "will stretch out" his hand and do what is promised (Ex. 3:20). This is an idea we'll return to often, but for now, understand that God doesn't call leaders *because they are strong*. He calls leaders *and makes them strong*.

So this sin, this fear of man, is something from which we can be set free. You and I don't have to be great because God is. In Psalm 150:2, we read, "Praise him for his mighty deeds; praise him according to his excellent greatness!" Instead of being rock star people who are brilliant enough to make an impact, we simply slip off our shoes, kneel, and say, "Here am I." It doesn't matter how big or small God's purpose for us seems. Why? Because it's His story for His glory. The pressure to impress people is off.

THE THREE SIGNS

God knew about this fear in Moses. So He gave him three signs to perform should the people doubt him. The first was the snake from the staff. The second was exchanging a leprous hand for a healed one. And the third miracle foreshadowed one of the great plagues, pouring water from the Nile and watching it transform into blood as it spattered on dry earth. These miracles signified a mastery over nature itself.

SECOND RELUCTANCE: ABILITY

Even after being armed with these signs, Moses still doubts. He tells God, "Oh, my Lord, I am not eloquent, either in the past or since you have spoken to your servant, but I am slow of speech and of tongue" (Ex. 4:10). This sets the LORD over the edge and kindles his anger "against Moses" (Ex. 4:14). But even here, God meets Moses in his deficiency. He continues in verses 14-17, saying: "Is there not Aaron, your brother...? I know he can speak well. Behold, he is coming out to meet you... You shall speak to him and put the words in his mouth, and I will be with your mouth and with his mouth and will teach you both what to do. He shall speak for you to the people, and he shall be your mouth, and you shall be as God to him. And take in your hand this staff, with which you shall do the signs."

Here, we learn the crux of godly leadership: *God gives his leaders their mission, gives them the words to speak, and teaches them how to accomplish what's before them.* As leaders, we simply look to God, listen to Him in intimacy, and obey His voice in faith. And to satisfy this truth further, God sends Moses with his staff as a memorial, a constant reminder that it's by His power the people will be freed.

THIRD RELUCTANCE: OBEDIENCE

Finally, Moses seems satisfied with God's gracious responses. Infused with purpose, he heads home to begin his work.

THE BRIDEGROOM OF BLOOD

However, it's here we see his third reluctance—and the most bizarre moment in his entire story.

After stopping by home, he takes his wife and children with him, heading back to Egypt. The LORD continues to speak with Moses along the way and gives him more details as to how events will unfold. He prepares Moses that he will "harden Pharaoh's heart, so that he will not let the people go" (Ex. 4:21). Then, He gives Moses a bone-chilling threat to level against the Pharaoh.

Now, Moses has a game plan, clear guidance, and the message he must deliver. He continues on, heading to meet Aaron and begin their mission. But on the way, a baffling thing happens: "At a lodging place on the way, the LORD met him and sought to put him to death" (Ex. 4:24).

This brief interlude of Moses's story has stumped people for ages. It seems so out of character, counterproductive, and even random to what God was doing through Moses. But if we take a peek beneath the hood, we do see something deeper going on here. We're witnessing an old sin, a reluctance to follow God's command even before his mission began.

Let's read all three verses of this interlude, then unpack what's going on: "At a lodging place on the way, the LORD met him and sought to put him to death. Then Zipporah took a flint knife and cut off her son's foreskin and touched Moses' feet with it and said, 'Surely you are a bridegroom of blood to me!' So he let him alone. It was then that she said, 'A bridegroom of blood,' because of the circumcision" (Ex. 4:24-26).

We have four characters involved. God is the aggressor.

THE MEN WITH BARE FEET

Moses is the mark. Zipporah, Moses's wife, is the upset surgeon. And their son, presumably their firstborn Gershom, who gets an impromptu surgery (we also don't know how old he is at the time). Now, we're given little picture of how God sought to kill him. Who knows if it was through a band of robbers, bloodthirsty animals, angels with giant swords, or a deathly sickness. Whatever the means, it was certainly terrifying. To get a more vivid picture, let's imagine what this could have looked like.

IMAGINE THIS SCENE

I can see Moses scrambling over rocky wilderness paths, running from the danger. His eyes wide with terror, screaming in fear as he went. Finally, he makes it to a lodge with his wife and sons. They burst through the door in a panic.

"What on earth is going on?" Zipporah asks.

Moses replies, "Something is after me, and it means to see me dead. I don't know if I'm going to make it, Zipporah."

She squints her eyes in anger and purses her lips. "I know exactly what this is about," she says.

"You do? How?" Moses asks. He slumps down to the ground, his back still against the outer wall of the tent.

Without speaking, she brandishes a flint knife. Moses is dumbfounded and watches as she falls to her knees, laying Gershom on the ground. The little boy starts crying and kicking his legs. Then, in quick succession she slices the toddler's foreskin off with the jagged stone knife. He screams in pain, tears streaming down in face. Moses's jaw drops, his mind swimming in confusion.

THE BRIDEGROOM OF BLOOD

Zipporah stands, knife in one hand, Gershom's foreskin in another. Blood drips from her fingers, and she reaches the cowering Moses in three strides. She kneels down and swipes the bloody foreskin across his feet. Leaving a scarlet streak as a witness to his disobedience to the God he'd just met. The one who'd required his feet be bare.

She shouts, "You're a savage husband of blood to me!"

The room is tense. Zipporah is fuming. Gershom writhes in pain. But realization dawns on Moses's face. He instantly knows that the threat to his life has evaporated. He's safe, and his family is now right with God. Zipporah cries, upset. Moses bandages his son, cradles his wife, and explains to her what just happened.

OBEDIENCE IS ALWAYS REQUIRED

Just before we read this wild story, God told Moses the threat he was going to deliver to Pharaoh. Moses was to speak for God, saying, "... If you refuse to let [my people] go, behold, I will kill your firstborn son" (Ex. 4:23). You see, God didn't simply think of the Israelites as subjects in His divine kingdom. Instead, they were His children, His sons and daughters. In effect, He was going to tell Pharaoh, "If you continue to kill my sons, I'm going to kill yours." Just like the Pharaoh before him, this man was evil, too. These weren't nice people who were simply in the wrong place at the wrong time. Remember, this was a dynasty who'd committed the infanticide that Moses narrowly escaped as a baby.

To this point, God had rooted His instructions to Moses in the covenant He'd made to Abraham more than

THE MEN WITH BARE FEET

500 years prior, in Genesis 12:1-3. Before they were ever in Egypt, God marked Abraham's descendants as His own. In Genesis 17, we learn yet another way He was going to do this. In that chapter, God shows Abraham something special he must do to his sons. It was to be a physical mark that separated Abraham's offspring from all other people, as part of God's "everlasting covenant" with them (Gen. 17:7). This rite was circumcision.

On the eighth day, every son of Abraham was to have his foreskin cut off in observance of the covenant. We don't have space to explore this painful command in depth, but here was the bottom line: *God said to do it so his people were to obey*. And this is a principle that perpetuates through the whole Bible, and the rest of this book. So, if we turn back to the interlude in Exodus, the necessity of circumcising Gershom makes a lot more sense.

It's obvious that Moses had never obeyed God's command and circumcised his firstborn son. So just like the threat to Pharaoh, this episode was a threat to Moses. If the king of Egypt couldn't get away with disobedience, neither could Moses. God's word is never optional. When He commands something, His people should obey. This was just as true of Moses. When we see the event in this light, an interesting grace twinkles from behind dark storm clouds.

God drove Moses, the man who would deliver the Law to his people, to obedience. He showed him the stakes of ignoring the covenant. It was evident that Zipporah wasn't thrilled with the rite of circumcision, so maybe Moses ignored it to keep the peace in his household? After all, we have already seen a pattern of fear in him. He would become one of history's most legendary leaders, but even he was scared of what people thought. And in this case, it must have been his wife's opinion of him that he feared more than God's.

LET'S GET ON WITH IT

Exodus 4 ends on a bright note. After the incident, Moses meets Aaron at Mt. Horeb, where he'd met Yahweh in the burning bush. Just as God said, Aaron is happy to see him (Ex. 4:14), and the two debrief on what the future holds. The newly christened leaders return to Egypt and gather the elders of Israel. Then, before their eyes, Moses performs the miracles God told him to. As a salve to his fear, he learns again that God was right: "And the people believed" (Ex. 4:31).

The people embrace Moses and Aaron because they felt the truth from chapter 2, verse 25, "God saw the people of Israel—and God knew." This line should've made the pyramids quake. Israel's Almighty Father saw the inhuman abuse, *and He knew*. Nothing the Egyptians did to them escaped Him. Every infant's death cry, every slaver's whip crack, every royal family curse, God knew it all.

Can you feel what an incredible moment this was?

Imagine the people's tears. Their sleepless nights beneath stars who witnessed constant cruelty. Days that bled one into another, crushed under oppression. Hoisting stones to build their masters' grand houses and tombs. Working diligently to beautify the nation that scarred their bodies. And now, after decades of abuse, the glorious truth of God's *knowing* blazed like fire. So, "they bowed their heads and worshiped" (Ex. 4:31).

THE MEN WITH BARE FEET

So began the greatest story of their lives. The story God started with a little boy floating in a basket. The same man He'd use to bring an empire to its knees. The one He'd empower to bury warriors in the sea just as they had done to Israel's sons. The story of a fearful man who met God with bare feet, saying a simple, "Here am I." The Exodus was now underway.

THE BRIDEGROOM OF BLOOD

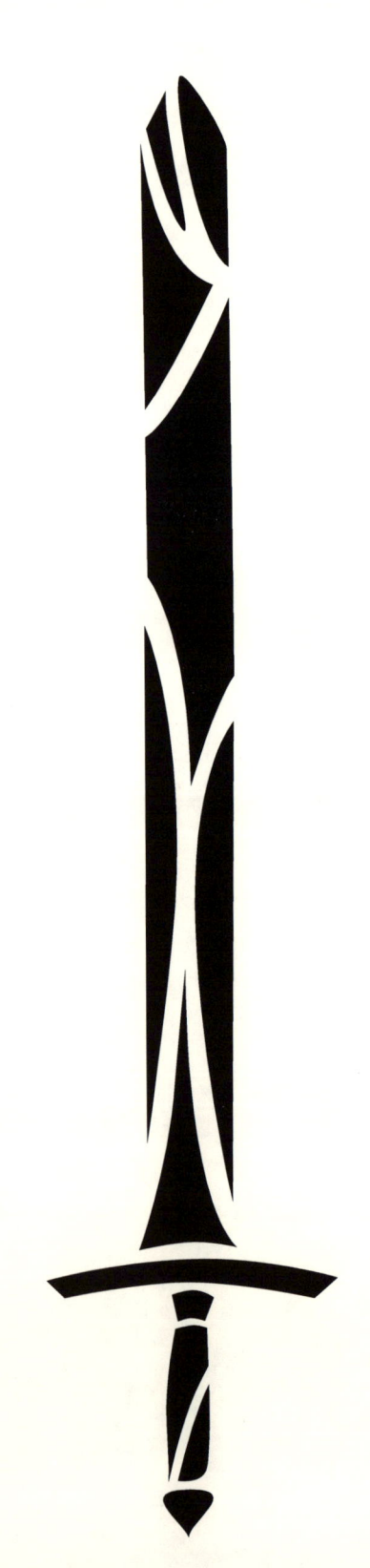

PART TWO
JOSHUA

FOUR

THE MOUNTAINSIDE APPRENTICE

REGARDLESS OF HIS ROCKY START, Moses proved to be one of God's most faithful leaders. He famously led the people out of Egypt, following God's visible presence as they fled. He manifested Himself in a column of flame by night and a cloud of glory by day. Then, God told Moses to stretch out his staff toward the Red Sea, making the waters roll back on themselves, creating a miraculous causeway for the people to cross. This path, of course, would become the Egyptian army's tomb.

Just as they had drowned Israel's children years before, God would drown their legions of warriors—a staggering warning statement that would resound throughout the land: God fights for and defends His people. From here, they journey farther into the wilderness. God performing other wonders through Moses's staff and

THE MEN WITH BARE FEET

sending manna from heaven to feed them. Though the people started to grumble and even came near to stoning Moses because they were angry (Ex. 17:4), a new test was marching their way—an army ready to wipe them out. In this chapter, we'll skip a stone across Moses's final years of leadership and meet his apprentice and eventual successor, Joshua. Here, we get an even deeper view of how God forges mighty leaders.

REPHIDIM

There was a king named Amalek who ruled the Amalekites. He mustered his army and attacked the Israelites at a place called Rephidim while en route to Mt. Sinai. Here, in Exodus 17:9, at the battle of Rephidim, we meet the second character of our book: Joshua.

Moses calls him into action, and we learn that he's a general and commander of their army. He assembles their force, barks out battle plans, and prepares for war. These tactics would be different than most wars, however. The best generals are the ones who play to their army's strengths. If they have excellent archers, they try to cut down the enemy before they're within swinging distance. If they have a cavalry that can role through tides of warriors like a hot sword through manna, then that's their central charge.

Israel's army had a different strength. To play to it, their forces would be split up, with one party overlooking the battle from the mountainside, and the other fighting the Amalekites sword-to-sword. But the battle party that marched up the hill was small, made of only Moses and two other men. These three weren't equipped with long-range weapons or even a way to direct their forces below. Instead, while Joshua charged with his sword, Moses would fight with his staff. He told Joshua, "I will stand on the hill with the staff of God in my hand" (Ex. 17:10).

The fight was brutal. Sometimes Israel prevailed, only to be pushed back by the Amalekites. However, the linchpin wasn't Joshua's skills as a tactician or his men's warring ability. What turned the tide was when Moses held his staff high above his head. But when his "hands grew weary" and the staff slumped down, the Amalekites rallied. Battle cries rang out, metal clanged against metal, and soldiers fell in heaps. But the skirmish turned to Israel's favor for good when the two men who went up with Moses, his brother Aaron and a man named Hur, helped him hold the staff aloft. They kept his hands "steady until the going down of the sun. And Joshua overwhelmed Amalek and his people with the sword" (Ex. 17:12-13). In surprising fashion, Moses and Joshua's first battle in Exodus is won—and it's because of God's supernatural influence.

I believe the following verse, though, is the most important in this passage. In our first introduction to Joshua, we learn he's a skilled man of war. But we also see the Lord preparing him for leadership. In verse 14, we read, "Then the LORD said to Moses, 'Write this as a memorial in a book and recite it in the ears of Joshua, that I will utterly blot out the memory of Amalek from under heaven.' "

Joshua was supposed to memorize God's promise and command. The Amalekites, an evil people, sought to destroy God's people. Justice would be done, but Joshua immediately learned the most crucial lesson of his military career. It was a truth Moses had already memorialized in his song of praise after they'd walked safely through the Red Sea. In Exodus 15:3, we hear Moses sing, "The LORD is a man of war; the LORD is his name."

Joshua experienced firsthand that God is the ultimate warrior. He is their strength, sword, and shield. No matter how far their warriors could hurl a spear... how deftly they could swing a sword... how mighty a blow they could withstand... the battle is God's alone, which means so is the glory.

WHAT IF YOU WERE THERE?
Try to put yourself on the front lines. Imagine squaring off against a trained military force on an arid plain. Your enemies unsheathe their swords, ready their bows, and rattle their spears. You hear their war drums pounding, deep booms ringing louder, growing more frenzied. Your palms are sweaty, and your breathing quickens. Sure, you're a trained warrior, too—and Joshua's skills are legendary. But your army's secret weapon is actually no weapon at all.

You glance back and see Moses, Aaron, and Hur take position high above. They look small and very far away. This is troubling, as you didn't simply run into a band of robbers in the desert. These people were actually *hunting* you. They were after your lives. As the general speaks, your attention is turned to the front of the ranks.

"Remember!" Joshua cries. "Remember the Nile running red with blood. Remember the pillar of fire and the cloud of glory. Remember the mighty waters that became walls for us to walk between. Remember the world's greatest army plunged into the sea on our heels. Remember who fights for us! Yahweh is a man of war; I AM is his name!"

Strength swells in your heart. Your ranks stir with energy. The incredible images of deliverance you have seen in the last months play through your mind. You remember who it is that's on your side. You remember who has called your people and made your path level thus far.

You turn back to Moses, surveying the battle field from his planned position. His staff looks like the smallest sliver of wood from here, but you smile. You know your enemy will fall before little more than a piece of drift wood. Joshua thrusts his sword forward, and your forces thunder ahead. The battle is just beginning, but you know it's already been won. The LORD has proven himself strong. Your job is simply to follow His lead. Moses may be far away, Joshua might be across the battlefield, but the real Hero is right by your side.

FIRE ON THE MOUNTAIN

After the victory at Rephidim, the people headed toward Mt. Sinai. This was the same mountain where Moses had met God in the burning bush. And now the glory he saw in miniature was about to be seen on a panoramic scale. When the people arrived at the base of the mountain, God told Moses what the days ahead held. And where did He speak from? He spoke to him from "out of the mountain" (Ex. 19:3). Moses was to tell the people: "You yourselves have seen what I did to the Egyptians, and how I bore you on eagles' wings and brought you to myself. Now therefore, if you will indeed obey my voice and keep my covenant, you shall be my treasured possession among all peoples, for all the earth is mine; and you shall be to me a kingdom of priests and a holy nation..." (Ex. 19:4-6).

God is going to make His people His *treasured possession*, something special and holy to Him. He has plans and designs for them. Something new was happening in the people. No longer were they slaves, they were treasures. They were safe in the hand of the Almighty. And just as Moses saw God in the flames, the people would see Him upon the mountain.

God told Moses that He was going to descend upon the mountain in three days. And when He did so, the people needed to have "limits... all around" the mountain set for them (Ex. 19:12). Remember God's words of warning to Moses in chapter 3? "Come no closer and remove your sandals, you are standing on holy ground." This same holy presence was coming again.

On the third day, as promised, the people were met with a terrifying sight. Thick clouds swirled about the peak of Mt. Sinai. Thunder crackled and peels of lightning snaked through the air. An ominous trumpet sounded, seeming to come from thin air. And as God's tangible glory fell, the mountain shook, barely able to withstand the weight. Human beings are dwarfed by mountains, and this mountain was consumed by God.

Moses led the people out of their camp, straight to the foot of the mountain. The earth trembled like an earthquake beneath their feet and smoke like a "kiln" swarmed the mountainside (Ex. 19:18). The angelic trumpet rose in

THE MOUNTAINSIDE APPRENTICE

a crescendo, almost deafeningly loud, and when Moses spoke, "God answered him in thunder" (Ex. 19:19).

WAR IN THE CAMP

God summoned Moses to join Him on the summit. He pressed up into the storm of God's glory, and here received the Ten Commandments, instructions for the tabernacle, for the ark of the covenant, and more. We also see the Lord draw Joshua further into His presence than ever before.

In Exodus 24:13-14, we read that Moses and his apprentice, Joshua, "went up into the mountain of God. And he said to the elders, 'Wait here for us until we return to you...' " They were on the mountain for 40 days and nights (Ex. 24:18). God continued speaking to Moses, and he recorded everything He said. As Moses and Joshua are immersed in God's presence above, however, the people were growing restless below. We find in Exodus 32:1 that: "When the people saw that Moses delayed to come down from the mountain, the people gathered themselves together to Aaron and said to him, 'Up, make us gods who shall go before us. As for this Moses, the man who brought us up out of the land of Egypt, we do not know what has become of him.' "

Here is the difference in godly leadership. The glory of the LORD is still streaming across the mountainside. Aaron had spoken for God. He'd seen the plagues. He'd led the people alongside of Moses every step of the way. But now, he complies with the people, leading them into idolatry. They made the infamous golden calf, worshiped it as the "god" who led them out of captivity, and Aaron built an altar before it (Ex. 32:4-5). The people worshiped through sexual acts from dawn until dusk.

They shouted so loudly, that up on the mountain, Joshua was alarmed and said, "There is a noise of war in the camp" (Ex. 32:17). But Moses's heart sinks, because he knows right away, "It is not the sound of shouting for victory or the sound of the cry of defeat, but the sound of singing that I hear" (Ex. 32:18). God's people had immediately broken covenant with Him. And just as they broke it, Moses hurled down the tablets that "were the work of God, and the writing was the writing of God" (Ex. 32:16; 19).

Here, Joshua learned another lasting lesson well summarized by the theologian Francis A. Shaeffer: "War is not the greatest evil to come upon a people."[1] Idolatry is, because the people were worshiping a god who could not save them, and therefore condemning themselves. In the end, this idolatry caused the deaths of about 3,000 people (Ex. 32:28).

FACE TO FACE

The brutal truth is that sin is so intrinsically tied to us as people that when God deals with sin, he must deal with the sinner. This is the reason for the atonement of Jesus, the reason a human had to bodily bear the punishment for sin. The Apostle Paul tells us in Romans 6:23a that, "The wages of sin is death..."

---

[1] Schaeffer, Francis A. *The Complete Works of Francis A. Schaeffer: A Christian Worldview.* Vol. 2, A Christian View of the Bible as Truth. Wheaton, IL: Crossway Books, 1985.

THE MOUNTAINSIDE APPRENTICE

Through the events at Sinai, we see sin is serious. It wasn't to be taken lightly, and there was a just penalty to be paid. However, these were just the beginnings of God's grand design for redemption. Nonetheless, Joshua was tempered as a leader like steel through events like these. But before we move on from Moses's leadership to Joshua's, we'll make one more stop.

You see, Joshua's apprenticeship to Moses wasn't simply in acting as a general for Israel. Nor was it as a spectator, taking notes from the sidelines. It was also in intimacy with God.

In Exodus 33:11, we read, "Thus the LORD used to speak to Moses face to face, as a man speaks to his friend. When Moses turned again into the camp, his assistant Joshua, the son of Nun, a young man, would not depart from the tent." Joshua was more than an observer or employee-in-training. He was a man who sought after God. He stood with Moses upon the mountain, surrounded by God's glory. And came down the rocky face a man with a hungry soul. A man who wouldn't leave the tent of meeting. He treasured the presence of God. Soaked in it, he longed to be with Him.

So the question for us isn't simply *what* we long for, but *whom*. Are we people who ache to be with God and near to Him? Or do we flit from golden calf to counterfeit altars and back again? As we continue to watch Joshua's life as a leader unfold, this question will be important to continually pose to ourselves.

But let me be clear on this question's purpose.

My intention isn't to guilt anyone toward a relationship

with the Lord. Instead, it's to invite you. Right now, imagine the contrast between a thundering cloud of lightning, fire, and glory and a handmade calf statue. How do they compare? Which swells with life, power, and strength? And which is inert, needing to be sculpted by the hands of men?

Remember who has met us, the great I AM, the one who wasn't fashioned by hands of men but fashioned men with His own hands. And not only is He glorious and holy, He has come near because you, just like the Israelites, are God's treasured possession. So don't let shame propel you into simply behaving better. Let God's invitation into genuine relationship with Himself pull you into experiencing Him, knowing Him—not just knowing about him.

This is the cornerstone upon which Joshua's impact was built: a craving for God Himself.

FIVE

WORSHIP AS WARFARE

MOSES DIES at the end of Deuteronomy (Deut. 34:5), and Joshua is chosen by God to take his place as leader. It says he was "full of the spirit of wisdom, for Moses had laid his hands on him" (Deut. 34:9). So, the mantle is passed from one of the greatest prophets and leaders God's people have ever seen to Joshua. If you were Joshua, how would you be feeling right now? What a legacy to follow.

The truth is, there simply is no man who could have followed Moses's leadership ability by his own power. Why? Because Moses didn't accomplish anything by *his own power* either. When we come to the opening passages of Joshua, who do we find speaking first? God.

This is another mark of a Godly and humble leader—and this is one of my biggest failings. I'm far more prone to speak than listen. Here, though, we hear God say to Joshua, "No man shall be able to stand before you all the days of your life. Just as I was with Moses, so I will be with you. I will not leave you or forsake you. Be strong and courageous, for you shall cause this people to inherit the land that I swore to their fathers to give them" (Josh. 1:5-6).

As we'll see in this chapter, Joshua did what Moses did. He listened to God and then did what He said. He was a man of the book, just as God told him to be: "This Book of the Law shall not depart from your mouth, but you shall meditate on it day and night, so that you may be careful to do according to all that is written in it. For then you will make your way prosperous, and then you will have good success" (Josh. 1:8).

Joshua was going to lead the people into the promised land, and on the cusp of this, they had arrived at the banks of the Jordan River. The night before they made their crossing, Joshua said to them, "Consecrate yourselves, for tomorrow the LORD will do wonders among you" (Josh. 3:5).

Indeed, He did.

BEFORE THE EYES OF THE PEOPLE

The entire nation of Israel lined the banks of the Jordan River. However, the river was flowing high, as it flooded during harvest season (Josh. 3:15). So with the river engorged and moving swiftly, Joshua called out orders for Levitical priests to carry the ark of the covenant about half-a-mile in front of the people. God's presence dwelt there and would lead them. And He promised that when the soles of the priests' feet dipped into the river, the water would immediately stop flowing.

The scene that followed was incredible—*and should sound incredibly familiar*. The priests went ahead as planned and upstream, the waters began to roll back on themselves. A waterfall cascaded in reverse, defying gravity and hurdling toward the clouds. A tower of water rose ever higher as an entire nation walked across a bone-dry riverbed that was flooded out moments before.

In Joshua 4:14, after the people had crossed over, we learn, "On that day the LORD exalted Joshua in the sight of all Israel, and they stood in awe of him just as they had stood in awe of Moses, all the days of his life." Leadership works differently within the household of God than in the kingdom of men. Joshua never promoted himself. He never clawed and scratched for praise or applause or showcased his own abilities. Instead, the LORD set him up as a leader.

While leadership is certainly a noble pursuit and high calling, it is not initiated by us. God calls leaders and equips them—even when they seem an odd choice, like Moses did. And to cement Joshua's position of authority and seal him with further approval, God explicitly showed the people He was with him just like He was with Moses. Remember the parting of the Red Sea? Of course you do, and so did they.

The people saw flashbacks of being chased between titanic walls of water by bloodthirsty chariots. They recalled defying incredible odds and escaping with their lives and plunder from Egypt. God marked Joshua with unquestionable authority and exalted him before the people. All Joshua had to do was pursue God, meditate on His words, and stay obedient.

After the people crossed over, they camped at a placed called Gilgal. Here they set up twelve stones as a memorial to God's faithfulness, one from each tribe. They were taken from the Jordan River itself and set as a way to remember what God did for the people there. They were to tell their children what they meant, and what the LORD had done (Josh. 4:6-7). Here, they were to make generational testimonies. Parents were to remind their children of what God had done in front of their eyes.

THE COMMANDER OF THE ARMY OF THE LORD

Now we enter a new season for the people. No longer are they eating manna, but they have the "fruit of the land" (Josh. 5:12). From here, God would use Joshua's military brilliance to take the promised land. And the coming decades would be filled with battles and campaigns. However, before their first conquest, the city of Jericho, the LORD would bring Joshua to a burning-bush moment of his own.

They were on the plain of Jericho, near the city. He had already dispatched two spies who infiltrated the city and gathered intelligence from Rahab, who lived in the city's massive walls. Not only did she keep them safe, but she said in Joshua 2:10-11: "For we have heard how the LORD dried up the water of the Red Sea before you when you came out of Egypt, and what you did to the two kings of the Amorites... whom you devoted to destruction...

And as soon as we heard it, our hearts melted, and there was no spirit left in any man because of you, for the LORD your God, he is God in the heavens above and on the earth beneath."

The events at the Red Sea had taken place over forty years ago, yet the people of Jericho still feared the Israelites because of it. God's fame spread across the land like a wildfire. So much so, that this woman sided with God and His people—and both she and her family were saved because of it.

With his spies' intelligence in hand, then, Joshua lead Israel toward Jericho. It was time to take this city. But on the way, Joshua "lifted up his eyes and looked, and behold, a man was standing before him with his drawn sword in his hand. And Joshua went to him and said to him, 'Are you for us, or for our adversaries?' " (Josh 5:13).

En route, he saw a man with his sword drawn, obviously poised for battle. Because Joshua didn't recognize him, he had to identify whether he was a friend or foe. But the man's response surprised him. He answered to Joshua, "No, but I am the commander of the army of the LORD. Now I have come" (Josh. 5:14).

He told Joshua that he was neither for Israel nor Jericho. Instead, he was *for God*. In saying this, he made something crystal clear: God is not on your side, you are on His. If you are aligned with God, then you war for Him. And if you war for Him, you serve me as the commander of His army.

Joshua's response was immediate: He "fell on his face to the earth and worshiped him and said to him, 'What does my lord say to his servant?' And the commander of the LORD's army said to Joshua, 'Take off your sandals from your feet, for the place where you are standing is holy.' And Joshua did so" (Josh. 5:14b-15).

Wow. Just as Moses met the LORD at the burning bush, Joshua met the commander of His army. But just who was this commander? I believe it was Jesus (a kind of theophany called a *christophany*, a manifestation of the pre-incarnate Christ). You see, if he was an angel, he would not have accepted worship (see Rev. 22:9). But here, Joshua fell to the ground and worshiped. He also instructs Joshua, just as the LORD had to Moses, to go barefoot because he was on holy ground.

It's compelling to note here that Joshua is the Hebrew form of Jesus, and means "Yahweh is salvation."

WEAPONS OF WORSHIP

Joshua joins the ranks of those in barefooted intimacy with God. He bows low in reverence and respect and discovers something we can all take to heart. Often we're stuck in a pattern of seeing every event with ourselves at the center. Joshua asked the commander, "Are you for us or our enemies?" When instead, he should have been answering that very question to the one he asked!

Just as the sun doesn't orbit the earth, neither does the universe orbit around us. When we view the world through a self-centered lens, our problems loom ever larger as God grows more distant. Here, Joshua is reoriented in a way that sloughs weight from his shoulders—ours, too.

When we live and lead with ourselves at center stage,

our hope must be in our own strength. In short, the shortcut to idolatry is when we hope in anyone or anything other than God Himself. This is not the mode of God-honoring leadership. The fruit of believing in God's mission rather than our own is liberating.

In Joshua 6, we see Israel take the fortified city of Jericho in curious fashion. Ironically, Joshua met Jesus with his sword drawn, ready for battle, and Jericho's wall crumbles without a manmade weapon of war brandished. Instead, we read that the people marched around the city for a week, being led again by the ark of the covenant and trumpets of ram's horns. Israel's army was led into battle by the Spirit of the Lord and instruments of worship. And on the seventh lap of the seventh day, the people gave a "great shout, and the wall fell down flat, so that the people went up in to the city, every man straight before him, and they captured the city" (Josh. 6:20).

Today, when we worship, we are at war. When we sing praise to God, we battle against the powers and principalities that would defy His glory. Because when we worship, we step barefooted into the presence of God, bowing in reverence before a throne with only One sitting atop. When we worship, we join the refrain of Revelation 4:8, sounding day and night in the courtroom of God: "Holy, holy, holy is the Lord God Almighty, who was and is and is to come!" Joshua worshiped Jesus, then went to war against God's enemies. So do we.

SIX

CLINGING TO GOD

"BE STRONG and courageous, for you shall cause this people to inherit the land that I swore to their fathers to give them" (Josh. 1:6). This verse gets a lot of press. It's printed on graduation cards and coffee cups, branded on shirts, and plastered on bumper stickers. But growing up, instead of motivating me to be like Joshua—*full of strength and courage*—it made me feel bad, because I wasn't like that at all.

You see, I looked at God's command to be strong and courageous as a command that came with little help to carry it out. I thought there must've been something special about Joshua that was missing in me. I wanted to be strong and courageous, but I still found myself fearful and hesitant. What was wrong with me? Why couldn't I get with it, lace up my battle boots, and start kicking the kingdom of darkness in the teeth?

THE MEN WITH BARE FEET

The reason is simple. It's one word, and it makes all the difference in the world. That word is context. When we see a verse emblazoned all by itself, it can be dangerous if we're not careful. Allow me to illustrate with Joshua 1:6 again:

"Be strong and courageous, for you shall cause this people to inherit the land that I swore to their fathers to give them."

Wow, God tells Joshua, "for you shall cause this people to inherit the land that I swore to their fathers..." That's a lot of pressure, isn't it? It seems like God's telling him, "Joshua, you'd better be tough and have some guts, because my covenant promise is all riding on you." But is this what God really meant? Without context, it might seem like it—but let's try again, now with verse 5 included as well:

> "No man shall be able to stand before you all the days of your life. Just as I was with Moses, so I will be with you. I will not leave you or forsake you. Be strong and courageous, for you shall cause this people to inherit the land that I swore to their fathers to give them."

Now, that makes more sense, doesn't it? God wasn't telling Joshua to be strong because the entire Abrahamic covenant rested on his shoulders. Instead, he told Joshua three colossal things that form the foundation for all of his leadership:

1. No enemy would stand in his way;
2. He would be with him exactly as He was with Moses;
3. and there would never be even a second where God wasn't completely with him.

Verse 6 wasn't a hollow command based on Joshua's ability. Instead, it was an encouragement stemming from the threefold promise of God's abiding strength. In essence, He calmed Joshua's nerves by telling him, "Joshua, I will never leave you hung out to dry." God had a purpose for Joshua's strength and courage, so He was the one who fueled it.

WHERE STRENGTH AND COURAGE ARE FOUND

Once I began to understand where Joshua's power would come from, it helped me draw closer to the Lord. Instead of a sense that I wasn't good enough to be used by God, I saw the glorious reversal. It's not about how strong, bold, or brilliant we are. God takes little people and uses them for mighty things. Joshua learned this as Moses's apprentice, on the battlefield and Rephidim, and on the mountainside.

Joshua's preparation to lead God's people was filled with displays of God's power and strength. So when God whispers in his ear, "I will never leave you or forsake you," he was secure. God was certainly going to use Joshua to fulfill His grand covenant promise, but it wasn't up to Joshua to have it all together. He had a role to play and responsibilities to fulfill. But the way he served would be upside down from what leadership usually looks like.

HOW WE SERVE

Let's read God's charge in Joshua 1:6-9:

> "Be strong and courageous, for you shall cause this people to inherit the land that I swore to their fathers to give them. Only be strong and very cou-

rageous, being careful to do according to all the law that Moses my servant commanded you. Do not turn from it to the right hand or to the left, that you have good success wherever you go. This Book of the Law shall not depart form your mouth, but you shall meditate on it day and night, so that you may be careful to do according to all that is written in it. For then you will make your way prosperous, and then you will have good success. Have I not commanded you? Be strong and courageous. Do not be frightened, and do not be dismayed, for the LORD your God is with you wherever you go."

Do you hear Joshua's main leadership tasks? Obey God's words. Say God's words. Meditate on God's words. Trust God's words.

The basis of Godly leadership is obedient faith. Joshua wasn't told to retreat and draw up master plans. He was told to be strong and courageous by consuming God's words just like food and water. Every single day, God invited Joshua to saturate himself in His promises. They would form him. They would steel his resolve. They would make things clear. Joshua was given a regimen of remembrance that would fuel obedience. And the fruit of obedience would be success.

CLING TO GOD
Obedience and careful meditation on God's word characterized Joshua's leadership. If you saw him today, he'd be the guy with a Bible that looks like it's been through a war

zone—because it had. He was a man of the Book, and he called Israel to be so as well.

At the end of Joshua's life, the LORD had given Israel peace in their land (Josh. 23:1). He knew that his death was creeping up, so he called all the people together and gave them his final address. Through his career as their leader, they had defeated 31 kings (Josh. 12:24) and now enjoyed peace with their neighbors. He'd carved up the land according to God's will and given each tribe of Israel their inheritance.

Within the span of this man's life, the people had escaped Egyptian slavery, wandered as nomads through the wilderness, and now occupied the land God had promised centuries before. He could have spent his final speeches listing his glorious victories, and no one would have begrudged him. After all, he was a very good leader. Instead, he told the people this: "Therefore, be very strong to keep and to do all that is written in the Book of the Law of Moses, turning aside from it neither to the right hand nor to the left... but you shall cling to the LORD your God just as you have done to this day" (Josh. 23:6, 8). He reminds them of the words God spoke to him on his first day in office: Be strong and obey. And not just that, but "cling" to God.

If you've ever seen a little boy or girl get scared near their mother or father, you have a great picture of this. What do they do? They immediately cling to their parent's leg. They wrap themselves around it with all of their might and don't let go until they feel safe. Just as children cling to their parents in fear, Joshua told the people to cling to God.

This is wonderful on so many levels. But what makes my soul sing is that it's impossible to cling to someone far away, isn't it? You cannot cling to anyone who's not right by your side. Joshua knew God too well to doubt where He'd be. He'd met God with his bare feet, had stood right before Him and worshiped. He'd been surrounded by swirling glory. He'd fought beneath a sun that stood still in suspended light (Josh. 10:13).

Joshua was unshakably confident in two realities: God's power and His nearness. God wasn't simply powerful, but far away. He wasn't close by, but weak. He was mighty and right by his side, because He never leaves nor forsakes His people. This is why Joshua gives the people a final ultimatum between false gods and Yahweh: "Now therefore, fear the LORD and serve him in sincerity and faithfulness. Put away the gods that your fathers served beyond the River and in Egypt, and serve the LORD... choose this day whom you will serve... But as for me and my house, we will serve the LORD" (Josh. 23:14-15).

Joshua knew that the idols of other nations would fail them. False gods, like their golden calf from Exodus 32, might seem near, but they are powerless. So Joshua reminds them of who the real God is. He reminds them of His power, proximity, and character. And, as their leader, commits himself and his family to God. In front of the entire nation, Joshua says that it's time to choose once and for all to whom you will cling.

And he made his choice clear.

THE GOD WHO CLINGS TO US

Now, as we leave Joshua's story and turn to a new one, let's view one more image to better understand Joshua's call.

CLINGING TO GOD

In Luke 15:11-32, Jesus tells the "Parable of the Prodigal Son." It's the story of two sons and their father. One son is a good boy. He does everything he's told, is wise with his inheritance, and sticks around home. The other son, however, isn't so good.

When he gets his money, he wasn't smart with it. Instead, he goes from city-to-city, partying, making bad friends and worse decisions, until one day he swiped his debit card to buy lunch and was told, "Sir, I'm sorry, but your card has been declined." He was broke.

Humiliated, ashamed, and starving, his new friends vanish. No one's there to help. So he gets a job at a pig farm. He's in charge of filling their troughs with the decaying slop and rotten food nobody else will eat. In fact, he was in such a desperate state that he fell to his knees in the mud and longed to eat the putrid slop splattered before him.

However, just as he was about to plunge his face into the grime and eat, he realized something. He said to the pigs nearby, "What am I doing? My father is a wealthy man, and all of the servants in his house have plenty to eat. Maybe he'll let me work for him as a servant?" Then, he left straight from the pig farm to his family's estate.

He was nervous to see his family again, his cheeks bright red with embarrassment. He rehearsed what he was going to say over and over in his mind. Then, he heard some noise up ahead. He looked, and there he was: his father. But before he could apologize or say anything to him, he hugged his son and kissed him. Even covered in slop, his father cried tears of joy at his return, accepted him back into his house as a full son, and gave him fresh clothes and food.

In this parable, Jesus is showing us God the Father's heart. He's showing His joy when His prodigal children return home. And He's showing us that not only can we cling to God, but He clings to us. Just as Joshua knew, God is near and brimming with love for us. Even when we have pig slop on our clothes or mud on our feet, we have a Father ready to embrace us and make us clean.

We cling to a God who clings to us.

CLINGING TO GOD

PART THREE
JESUS

SEVEN

THE SERVANT'S BASIN

So far, this book has been an exploration of what made Moses's and Joshua's impact so potent. The answer has been simple: God. We've seen His nature on mountainsides and battle fields. We've seen Him intervene in miracle after miracle, paving His people's path to freedom. But our theme of intimacy still feels a little unsatisfied, doesn't it? If we can't meet Him in a swirling cloud or see His hand stopping the tides, how can we experience the closeness those men did?

Well, we have one more story to explore, and one more man to consider. Hebrews 1:3 says that this man "is the radiance of the glory of God and the exact imprint of his nature…" Paul writes in Colossians 2:9, "For in him the whole fullness of deity dwells bodily, and you have been filled in him, who is the head of all rule and authority."

THE MEN WITH BARE FEET

This man is Jesus.

Let's pause here for a moment. If what Paul says is true, then we are *filled* with the glorious God of the Sinai tempest. I can't get that picture out of my mind. The image of that craggy peak, wreathed in glory, an entire nation looking on. A holy presence once unapproachable *now dwells inside of us*. Is it just me, or does your heart leap to think about the power of I AM living in you?

If this is true, which I believe it is, it changes everything. Absolutely everything. What do we have to fear when this God has made us His temple? Do we need to fear people, like Moses did? Do we need to rush into battle, checking at the last second to see if the Lord's on our side, like Joshua did? No. Let's spend these final pages exploring the infinite God who makes His home in finite people. Let's behold Jesus, who's the clearest picture of who God is, what He's like, and what He cares about in the world.

THE SERVANT'S BASIN

In John 13, we find our final barefoot encounter. The same God who burned before Moses and brandished a sword before Joshua washes dust and dung from His disciples' feet. The radius of holy fire is gone. And now, Jesus doesn't command the disciples to remove their sandals because of the ground they stand on. In a stunning reversal, He kneels and washes the filth from their feet by hand.

They were eating supper when this happened. And in those days, they didn't sit on chairs and at tables like we do. They reclined on cushions, propped up on an elbow. This meant that messy, sandaled feet were rude and unhygienic.

Because of their sandals, people's feet would be caked with dirt or feces from animals. Usually, washing guests' feet was a servant's job. So you can imagine the disciples' surprise when Jesus knelt down to work.

In fact, it would have even been slightly embarrassing. Imagine if you were in a similar culture, about to eat dinner with an important dignitary. It's someone whom you respect, admire, and even want to emulate. In fact, they're so important to you that you'd give up just about anything to spend time with this person. However, when you arrive with messy feet, he or she kneels down and serves you.

A PLEA FOR NEEDINESS

That's such an uncomfortable thought, isn't it? It was for Peter, too. When Jesus came to wash his feet, Peter said, "You shall never wash my feet" (Jn. 13:8). It sounds so noble, and even right, doesn't it? The master doesn't serve the apprentice, it's the other way around. But pay careful attention to Jesus's reply. He answered to Peter, "If I do not wash you, you have no share with me" (Jn. 13:9).

Jesus showed the disciples, and now us, that we should be needy, not noble. None of us can come to Jesus believing we don't need washed. Just as Paul wrote in Titus 3:4-7: "But when the goodness and loving kindness of God our Savior appeared, he saved us, not because of works done by us in righteousness, but according to his own mercy, by the washing of regeneration and renewal of the Holy Spirit, whom he poured out on us richly through Jesus Christ our Savior, so that being justified by his grace we might become heirs according to the hope of eternal life."

THE MEN WITH BARE FEET

We come to Jesus not because we are worthy, but because of our desperation. My plea to you is to rebuke the streak of independence in yourself, that place of pride that whispers to Jesus, "You shall never wash my feet," because of some misguided nobility.

This is barefooted discipleship. Intimacy with God begins by laying yourself open. Ask to be filled rather than pretending you already are. You see, we don't flatter God by needing Him. We don't pray to Him or study His Word to make Him feel nice and needed, like a mom whose children are grown. Instead, we are like those little Israelite baby boys in this world. Cruelly being carried to the Nile's edge, near to being thrown helpless into the water. What good would it be to pretend otherwise?

When Jesus washed the disciples' feet, it was an invitation to need Him. Jesus closed the gap between us and God's holiness by making us holy through His blood on the cross. Because of His atonement, when the Father looks at us, He sees Jesus. He sees disciples with feet cleaned by Jesus, not children tracking mud on the carpet that He's agreed to put up with. He loves us as He loves his son, because we are in Him.

This intimate exchange also provided an example for how we are to lead. He said to them, "Do you understand what I have done to you? You call me Teacher and Lord, and you are right, for so I am. If I then, your Lord and Teacher, have washed your feet, you also ought to wash one another's feet" (John 13:12-14).

Just as He meets our needs, we are to meet one another's.

THE SERVANT'S BASIN

BOOKENDED BY BETRAYAL

Near the end of the chapter, in John 13:34-35, Jesus delivers well-known words: "A new commandment I give to you, that you love one another: just as I have loved you, you also are to love one another. By this all people will know that you are my disciples, if you have love for one another." These words are convicting to me, and I wish I loved my brothers and sisters in Christ far better than I do. But, if you can imagine, they're even more convicting when you read this new commandment in context.

Just a few verses earlier, in John 13:27, Jesus told Judas Iscariot, "What you are going to do, do quickly." Judas was on his way to betray Jesus for some silver. Jesus knew this. He wasn't in the dark. He shared a meal with His betrayer; and not only that, but He'd just washed his feet. And how would He do it? Sealed with a kiss, the sign of peace. Even after this, He still commands us to love one another, as He loves.

If this wasn't bad enough, though, we have John 13:38, the final verse in this chapter. Just on the heels of this glorious pronouncement of love, Jesus prophesies Peter's betrayal. Jesus asked him, "Will you lay down your life for me? Truly, truly, I say to you, the rooster will not crow till you have denied me three times."

Betrayed by Judas, denied by Peter. All of this, and yet He loved the disciples to the end (Jn. 13:1), and commanded us to do the same. We could never love this way on our own strength, however. To be a disciple who reflects our Master means intimacy married with obedience.

THE MEN WITH BARE FEET

EIGHT

LIVING WITH BARE FEET

ONE OF THE MOST PROFOUND BOOKS I've ever read is J.I. Packer's *Knowing God*. He begins one chapter with these words: "What were we made for? To know God. What aim should we set ourselves in life? To know God. What is the 'eternal life' that Jesus gives? Knowledge of God...What is the best thing in life, bringing more joy, delight, and contentment than anything else? Knowledge of God...What, of all the states God ever sees man in, gives Him most pleasure? Knowledge of Himself."[1]

These words have stirred me for years and always rung true. What could be more valuable than God? Nothing. So, to examine my life against this, I've started asking, "What is the fruit of knowing God?" That's a

---

[1] Packer, J. I. *Knowing God*. Downers Grove, IL: InterVarsity Press, 1973.

pretty broad question, but I've narrowed it down to two primary indicators. So in this final chapter, I'll share this conviction. I'm convinced intimacy and obedience are the fountainheads of true discipleship.

TRUE DISCIPLESHIP

Intimacy means both *knowing* someone and *being known* by them. This works the same way with God, and it's apparent that this is Jesus's desire for us. In John 17:3, Jesus prayed: "And this is eternal life, that they know you the only true God, and Jesus Christ whom you have sent." And earlier, in John 10:27, He said that His sheep hear His voice, He *knows* them, and they follow Him.

Paul plucks this golden thread and weaves it through his epistles as well. He talks of being "fully known" by God (1 Cor. 13:12) and is floored that the Galatians, who have come to both "know God" and "be known by God" have turned away from the Gospel (Gal. 4:9). To be intimate with God means that He is revealed to us, and we to Him. He gives us full access to Himself, and in turn, we don't hide from Him. We invite him to search and know us, leading us in the "way everlasting" (Ps. 139:23-24).

THE BRIDE

As Christians, we must understand that eternal life is not something that begins in a far-off place called heaven, a place we are invited to if we don't do bad stuff now so we get something good later. Eternal life begins in relationship with God Himself—not a cheap, candy-coated, buzzword, lip-service-only relationship. But one that progressively deepens, grows richer, and more complete like a Groom and his Bride. Remember: "When one turns to the Lord, the veil is removed. Now the Lord is the Spirit, and where the Spirit of the Lord is, there is freedom. And we all, with unveiled face, beholding the glory of the Lord, are being transformed into the same image from one degree of glory to another. For this comes from the Lord who is the Spirit" (2 Cor. 3:16-18).

Wow. Just like a bride removes her veil on her wedding day, the Lord tore the veil that separated us from His presence, making us His ark, His tabernacle, His temple. Intimacy is both the disciple's secret and great right. Disciples aren't first marked by *what they do, but by who they're with*. Their actions are the fruit of that Master-disciple relationship. Fruit tells the story, but is never where it begins.

Think about it like this. Even though Peter tragically denied Jesus on that cold, dark night, how did people identify him as a disciple? A relative of Malchus (the guy whose ear Peter lopped off) recognized him as one of the people "in the garden with" Jesus (Jn. 18:26).

DISCIPLES DEFINED

Disciples are people who sit at their Master's feet. They follow Him, live with Him, emulate Him. They are commissioned by their Master after learning the essence of His way. One of my favorite college professors, Dr. John L. Hiigel, wrote something that has always stuck with me: "When we ask about how to live as disciples, we find not a topical essay or a set of instructions, but a story." [2]

This is important to understand, especially when considering verses like 1 John 2:6: "Whoever says he abides in [Jesus] ought to walk in the same way in which he walked." Does John mean Jesus's disciples simply need to do the things that Jesus did? In part, yes. But the whole is deeper.

Actions may speak louder than words, but they only sparkle with eternity when springing from relationship with the Eternal Word. To walk like Jesus walked means to become like Him in heart and spirit. It is sitting at Jesus's feet with such intimacy—*and regularity*—that we operate from "the mind of Christ" (1 Cor. 2:16).

The Master we serve determines the disciples we become. And how did the Twelve (minus the traitor) set the world ablaze? They were first lit afire by the One who baptized with the Holy Spirit and fire (Matt. 3:11); the same Holy Spirit later fanned those flames (Acts 2:3). The same Holy Spirit that lives in us, uniting us with God Himself, and intimately knitting our hearts together with one another.

OBEDIENCE

In John 4, the disciples were flummoxed when they returned to the well at Sychar only to find Jesus talking to a lady that, culturally, He shouldn't be. Still more odd is that when they urged Him to eat, He declined, saying He had other food they didn't know about.

---

[2] Hiigel, John L. Partnering with the King: Study the Gospel of Matthew and Become a Disciple of Jesus. Brewster, MA: Paraclete Press, 2013.

They were confused and wondered if someone else had already fed Him. But Jesus surprised them, saying, "My food is to do the will of him who sent me and to accomplish his work..." There it is. Jesus's fuel was obedience. We see this motif again and again in his ministry:

- He only does and says what He sees the Father doing and saying (John 5:19; 8:28; 12:49);
- He bends His will to the Father's in ultimate sacrifice (Luke 22:42);
- And even though He is the Son, He still learned obedience through suffering (Heb. 5:8).

In fact, the only childhood story beyond His birth that we have shows Him telling his parents, "Why were you looking for me? Did you not know that *I must* be in my Father's house?" (Lk. 2:49; emphasis mine). Jesus wholeheartedly embodied Samuel's prophecy to King Saul, that "to obey is better than sacrifice, and to listen than the fat of rams" (1 Sam. 15:22). Remember the context of that passage?

God had called Saul to "utterly devote" the Amalekites "to destruction." They were to wipe out all the people and all of their stuff as a judgment against them (remember the words Joshua was given in Exodus 17:14). So, Saul takes an army and routes them. But does he obey? Was he a leader like Moses or Joshua?

Not at all. Instead, he takes their king, Agag, and their "choicest" possessions as trophies—fat cattle, extra-fluffy sheep, and other valuables. When Samuel confronts him about this, what is Saul's rationale? He doesn't repent, instead he defends himself and says, "I obeyed God and completed the mission He sent me on. In fact, I kept some of the best stuff so that I could *worship* God by sacrificing these fineries to Him" (1 Sam. 15:20-21).

In this story, we see Israel's leader disobeying God and using worship as an excuse. Saul dressed up his sin in an ephod of righteousness. Does this sound like the spirit found in some of the people who Jesus would talk about centuries later? In Matthew 7:15-23, he warned: "Beware of false prophets. They come to you in sheep's clothing, but inwardly they are ravenous wolves. By their fruit, you will recognize them... A good tree cannot bear bad fruit, and a bad tree cannot bear good fruit... Many will say to me on that day, 'Lord, Lord, did we not prophesy in Your name, and in Your name drive out demons and perform many miracles?' Then I will tell them plainly, 'I never knew you; depart from me, you workers of lawlessness.' "

What's scary is that casting out demons, prophesying, and performing miracles in Jesus's name sounds *a lot* like what disciples are supposed to do. It looks a lot like right worship, doesn't it? Chilling. Intimacy with God and obedience to Him are intrinsically tied. Because to genuinely worship God first starts with knowing Him, and to obey is the measure of fruitfulness. Faith without works may be dead, but works without faith is digging one's own grave.

Think about Noah. By normal standards, he is the worst preacher of all time. Who responded to his message of the coming flood? Only seven other people—and they were all related to him. But what is the fruit of that obedience in the face of rejection? The salvation of the world.

BAREFOOTED DISCIPLESHIP

Moses learned to trust God despite his fear of what people thought of him. Joshua learned that strength and courage come from clinging to God in His nearness. And Jesus shows us that we are loved in a more intimate way than we ever thought possible.

To follow the men with bare feet means to drop our façades. It means to look at the God beside us rather than the situation around us. It means to cling to the God who clings to us. And when we draw close to this God, our faces will radiate His glory.

ABOUT THE AUTHOR

JORDAN IS AN AUTHOR AND SPEAKER with one love: teaching the Bible. And his favorite way to do so is by making its stories come alive. He has spoken at universities, as well scores of churches, retreats, and workshops. Each stage, lectern, and pulpit has reinforced his belief that what we all need most is Jesus.

When not writing, Jordan plays the drums and piano, loves to go on adventures in the mountains, adores reading G.K. Chesterton, and can't get enough of his wife and daughter. He holds a B.A. in theology/philosophy from the University of Sioux Falls.

Web: jordanloftis.com
Email: hello@jordanloftis.com
Phone: (303) 928-0876

NOTES

THE MEN WITH BARE FEET

NOTES

THE MEN WITH BARE FEET

NOTES

THE MEN WITH BARE FEET

NOTES